MEDITATION FOR BEGINNERS

HOW TO MEDITATE FOR PEOPLE WHO HATE TO SIT STILL

NTATHU ALLEN

Copyright © 2018 by Ntathu Allen.

All Rights Reserved.

No part of this book may be reproduced, stored in retrieval systems, or transmitted by any means, electronic, mechanical, photocopying, recorded or otherwise without written permission from the author.

ISBN: 978-1-63161-062-2

Published by TCK Publishing

www.TCKPublishing.com

Get discounts and special deals on our best selling books at

www.TCKPublishing.com/bookdeals

Health Disclaimer

This book and related sites provide wellness management information in an informal and educational manner only, with material that is general in nature and not specific to you, the reader. The contents of this site are intended to assist you and other readers in your personal wellness efforts. Consult your physician regarding the applicability of any information provided in our books and websites.

Nothing in this book should be construed as personal advice or diagnosis and must not be used in this manner. The information provided about conditions is general in nature. This information does not cover all possible uses, actions, precautions, side-effects, or interactions of medicines or medical procedures. The information in this book should not be considered as complete and does not cover all diseases, ailments, physical conditions, or their treatment.

You should consult with your physician before beginning any exercise, weight loss, or health care program. This book should not be used in place of a call or visit to a competent health-care professional. You should consult a health care professional before adopting any of the suggestions in this book or before drawing inferences from it.

Any decision regarding treatment and medication for your condition should be made with the advice and consultation of a qualified health care professional for treatment.

FREE GIFT FOR READING THIS BOOK

Visit: **www.YogaInspires.co.uk**

Get More Energy 7 Simple Stretches to Boost Your Energy. Free Guide Download with Video and Audio:
www.yogainspires.co.uk/subscribe

CONTENTS

Preface	*1*
Introduction	*5*
Chapter 1: What Is Meditation?	*9*
Chapter 2: Why Meditation Is Good for Your Health	*13*
Chapter 3: Most Common Obstacles People Face	*17*
Chapter 4: Mistakes to Avoid When Meditating	*25*
Chapter 5: A Simple Guide to Meditate with Ease	*31*
Chapter 6: The Easiest Way to Meditate	*35*
Chapter 7: Quick & Easy Ways to Meditate	*39*
Chapter 8: Special Bonus Section	*43*
Conclusion	*63*
About the Author	*65*

Preface

I want to thank *and* congratulate you for downloading *Meditation for Beginners: How to Meditate for People Who Hate to Sit Still.*

Did you know that in the UK 526,000 workers suffer from work-related stress, depression, or anxiety, and in 2016/2017, 12.5 million working days were lost to work-related stress, depression, or anxiety? Check this link for the statistics **www.hse.gov.uk/statistics/causdis/stress**.

If you have a hectic work schedule, I'm sure these figures don't shock you. Work overload, tension between colleagues, fear of job loss, financial difficulties, and personal relationship issues can leave you feeling drained, exhausted, and running on empty while you lie awake at night trying to find solutions. And when you eventually do fall asleep, you wake up feeling lethargic, fatigued, and anxious about the day ahead.

This constant spiral of feeling nervous, low on energy, and having your mind racing through possibilities leaves you feeling angry, frustrated, and concerned about your ability to cope.

Have you ever wondered what it would be like to start your day feeling energised, focused, and alert so that you have bags of energy during the day and can sleep soundly at night?

Would you like to have more certainty, confidence, and the belief that things will work out, that you are okay, and that your best is good enough?

Most people have heard about meditation as a way to deal with the stressful pace of daily life. But despite the growing popularity of meditation in the corporate and business world, as mentioned in this article from CNN

MEDITATION FOR BEGINNERS

(www.edition.cnn.com/2015/07/22/health/meditate-at-work/index.html), very often people struggle to make meditation a daily habit, or to even just get started. They feel meditation is too hard, is not for people like them; they are too busy, have too much to do, and they just can't sit still.

If this sounds like you, then *Meditation for Beginners, How to Meditate for People Who Hate to Sit Still* will help you gain a better understanding of meditation and how it can help you relax, reduce stress, and feel calm even if you can't sit still or if you struggle to calm your mind. Even if you are completely new to meditation or simply curious to discover more about how meditation can help you slow down, get stuff done, and enjoy good health this book was written just for you.

After reading this book, and practicing the guided meditations and breathing awareness exercises, you'll know how to quickly meditate for instant calm, clarity, and confidence.

The book is divided into two sections.

SECTION ONE:

Gives you a solid introduction into the theoretical side of meditation.

Topics covered include: what is meditation, the benefits of meditating, the common mistakes and obstacles most beginners face when meditating, and healthy habits you can adopt to meditate with ease.

You'll also be provided with a simple seven-step Meditation for Beginners checklist you can follow to help you meditate with ease. Even if you struggle to relax, calm your mind, or sit still, you'll still be able to use this checklist!

SECTION TWO:

At the end of the book, as a special bonus to help you relax even further and to enhance your meditation practice there are:

- Four simple guided breathing meditation techniques for beginners
- Three yoga breathing practices
- Seven meditation techniques specifically for people who hate to sit still!

And, for any stressed-out parents, I've also included two yoga breathing exercises especially designed for you to practice with your children! (So they can also experience the calming benefits of meditation from an early age and to give you both the perfect way to unwind at the end of a long day!)

All the meditations in this book are designed for you to use anywhere, anytime you feel:

- Scattered and overwhelmed by the 101 things on your to-do list
- Tired at the end of a busy day at work
- Low on energy and need a quick burst of energy to be more creative, alert, and productive at home and at work

The more you practice the suggested meditation techniques, the easier it becomes for you to:

- Overcome feeling overwhelmed and reduce stress
- Face the obstacles of life in a more relaxed, positive, and cheerful manner
- Gain a sense of calm, clarity, and sense of ease in all you do
- Have more energy and zest for living
- Feel happy, healthy, and productive during your day

MORE INFORMATION AND EXTRA RESOURCES

To support your preferred learning style, I have included references to articles, infographics, and videos from other bloggers and sources online.

To summarise, *Meditation for Beginners* is your starting point to help you learn how to:

1. Relax
2. Calm your mind
3. Meditate with ease following a simple seven-step formula, even if you struggle to sit still!

My dream is that you'll feel inspired by these meditations and (even if you hate to sit still) want to make meditation part of your daily routine for a happy, healthy, and more harmonious life.

Have a great day!

Ntathu Allen

Introduction

WHO I AM

My name is Ntathu Allen. I run the blog *Yoga Inspires.* The purpose of my blog is to support, encourage, and help busy people like you understand the basic elements of yoga and meditation as a way to learn how to relax, boost your energy, and reduce stress in your daily life, which means you'll feel happier, healthier, and have more energy to handle life's ups and downs.

HOW I GOT INTO YOGA AND MEDITATION

I first experienced yoga in 1991, while pregnant with my eldest daughter. My midwife was concerned about my health because I was stressed and exhausted from working as a full-time probation officer in a challenging inner city borough of London. She recommended I take up yoga and learn how to relax. I was too busy to go to classes, so I bought a couple of books and a relaxation tape but didn't do much until I was on maternity leave and started ante-natal classes to learn "how to relax."

In 1993 I had twin daughters.

Life became a blur of activity.

It was a relentless whirlwind of working, advancing up the career ladder, caring for my family, and trying to cope with the aftereffects of a miscarriage (1992), the sudden death of my cousin Sherry in 1995, and of my brother John in 1997. I was burnt-out.

I couldn't carry on mindlessly rushing around, putting out fires, and having no time, space, or energy to breathe—let alone think!

To cut a long story short… my work suffered, and my supervisor suggested I have bereavement counselling.

During the sessions, my counsellor suggested I practice breathing exercises and eventually meditation as a way to help me relax, reduce my internal stress levels, and—most important—help me sleep. I was having trouble sleeping because I had tight chest pains and struggled to breathe during the day, especially when I felt under pressure at work. It took me awhile to get the hang of meditating because my mind was sooooooooooooo busy and I couldn't sit still. I thought I was being lazy; I had so much other more important stuff to do. However, with support and guidance from my counsellor and other spiritual teachers I met along the way, I persevered and meditation—and now yoga—became part and parcel of my daily routine.

In 2000, I participated in an intense 12-month personal and spiritual development course that included daily yoga and meditation practice.

In 2003, inspired by the changes meditation and yoga made to my wellbeing, I followed a yearning deep inside for "change" and travelled to Kerala in India for six weeks to train as a Sivananda yoga teacher. This meant leaving my young daughters behind with my husband for six weeks.

In 2004, I resigned my secure, but stressful job as a probation officer to become self-employed and work as a yoga teacher. At that time, I was very naïve about the nuts and bolts of running my own business. I often look back now and think, how did I have the courage and faith to take such a step? And the answer is always the same—meditation. My daily meditation practice helps me stay focused, pick myself up when I'm down, and motivates and inspires me to show up day in, day out, building my business and following my dream. And now, that calling, that faith, has led me here, sharing what I know about meditation in this book. How cool is that?

Everything you read in *Meditation for Beginners* is based on my personal practice and on my teaching yoga and meditation to other super-busy women—most over 50 years old. These women are stressed out and want to live calm, healthy, and happy lives and find ways to relax, enjoy inner peace, and feel better so they can stop rushing around feeling overwhelmed and instead begin to embrace and enjoy a more peaceful and simpler way of living.

INTRODUCTION

Everything you read in this guide is based on my personal yoga journey and meditation practice plus my more than 12 years' experience teaching yoga and meditation to corporate organisations, community groups, and private one-on-one yoga at home lessons in South-East London.

Go to this link for more information on my private lessons: **www.yogainspires.co.uk/private-yoga-lessons-southeast-london**.

I also share my love of writing, yoga, and meditation in my book, *Yoga for Beginners: A Simple Guide to the Best Yoga Styles and Exercises for Relaxation, Stretching, and Good Health*.

In *this* book, *Meditation for Beginners*, you will learn:

- What meditation is and why meditation is good for your health
- Seven common signs of stress and its dangers
- Why meditation is good for your physical, emotional, and mental wellness
- The benefits of meditation on your brain waves
- The four most common obstacles meditation beginners face when they meditate and what you can do to overcome them
- The power of your breath as an aid in meditation to help reduce stress
- Five common mistakes most people make when they meditate and how to overcome them
- The seven-step process you need to follow to quickly meditate with ease

SPECIAL BONUS

- Four meditate-with-ease guided breathing meditation practices for beginners
- Three yoga breathing exercises—plus two child-friendly fun yoga breathing exercises you can practice with your children
- Seven meditation techniques for people who hate to sit still

Shall we begin?

What Is Meditaion?

To start, let's talk a bit about "meditation."

Let me offer an overview of meditation to give you the flavour, depth, and breadth of what meditation is.

Most people have an idea or image of what meditation is about.

Maybe you have seen the movie and read the book *Eat, Pray, Love* by Elizabeth Gilbert.

When I saw the movie, I sat mesmerised by Elizabeth Gilbert's spiritual journey through India and marvelled as she gained a deeper understanding, connection, and acceptance of herself through meditation and prayer.

Or, perhaps you have read blogs or popular magazines that feature top celebrities and entrepreneurs who regularly meditate.

For example, in the blogs, *Why The Most Famous People Meditate, and 17 Insanely Successful Celebrities Who Meditate Daily,* celebrities and politicians share how meditation helps them maintain their level of success and what meditation means to them.

Whilst doing my research for this section, I came across many definitions and explanations that address the question "What is meditation?"

One of the clearest descriptions is offered by the blogger and meditation teacher Giovanni Dienstman of the blog *Live and Dare*.

In his article, "What is Meditation and How to Start," Giovanni states:

> *Meditation is a mental exercise of regulating attention. It is practiced either by focusing attention on a single object, internal or external (focused attention meditation) or by paying attention to whatever is predominant in your experience in the present moment, without allowing the attention to get stuck on any particular thing (open monitoring meditation).*

Thus, there are two modes of meditation: concrete (known as saguna), and abstract (nirguna). In concrete meditation, you focus on an image, a picture, or other external object. For example, you might focus on a rose or a religious or spiritual image.

In abstract form of meditation, you meditate on an idea or concept, such as love, beauty, or peace.

For beginners, it is easier to focus your meditation on an image or external object, or something you can physically feel, like your breath or mala beads. Meditating on an abstract idea or concept such as divine love, loving kindness, or peace takes a greater level of skill and concentration.

Whether you practice seated or active meditation and your focus is inward or external, the key is to train your mind to concentrate on your point of focus and, as you deepen your practice and start to meditate, you sink into stillness and silence.

The word "meditate" means to think deeply about something.

However, as Giovanni tells us, when eastern contemplative practices were "imported" to Western culture, meditation (for lack of a better word) was the term used to define those practices.

"…nowadays meditation has more the meaning of this exercise of focusing attention than to reflect deeply."

Giovanni's explanation highlights the difference between the word "meditate" and the techniques we use to meditate. Meditation is a skill and you use different techniques to help you meditate.

And, Swami Rama, in his detailed article, "The Real Meaning of Meditation," states:

> *Meditation is a precise technique for resting the mind and attaining a state of consciousness that is totally different from the normal waking state. It is the means for fathoming all the levels of ourselves and finally experiencing the center of consciousness within. Meditation is not a part of any religion; it is a science, which means that the process of meditation follows a particular order, has definite principles, and produces results that can be verified.*
>
> *...In meditation, the mind is clear, relaxed, and inwardly focused. When you meditate, you are fully awake and alert, but your mind is not focused on the external world or on the events taking place around you. Meditation requires an inner state that is still and one-pointed so that the mind becomes silent. When the mind is silent and no longer distracts you, meditation deepens.*

MY PERSONAL UNDERSTANDING OF MEDITATION

During my meditation teacher training course, we were taught that meditation is like observing the sea on a calm and clear day. When you sit to meditate you see beyond the horizon and grasp a glimpse of your infinite potential and the vastness of the world.

During meditation you "travel inwards" and, with practice, you are able to fully experience a deep sense of calm, clarity, and conscious connection with all humanity.

And, whilst training to be a yoga teacher, in the Sivananda Yoga Teachers Training Course in Kerala, India, we had daily theoretical and practical lessons in meditation.

I still recall that feeling of awe and the sense of connection I felt sitting with the other yoga students and teachers. There were people from every corner of the globe, from all faiths, ages, and religions, and we were sitting together in silence, practicing meditation.

It was such an eye-opener for me to experience that depth of connection with such a diverse group of individuals. Learning to relax and meditate is a simple way to bring a sense of harmony, ease, and flow to your life.

As a black woman living and growing up in South East London, racism is rife and, up to that point, my worldview was seen through the lens of being black and a woman living in a predominately white male-dominated culture.

Yet, sitting there in silent meditation, I sensed that connection and finally understood what it means "to live as one." To be at peace and sense the infinite potential inside myself and others; to see beyond my neighbours' race, skin colour, faith, and economic status and connect with them through their breath. It was a total life changing moment for me to have that depth and sense of connection with people who had different beliefs and looked different from me. I deeply understood what my teachers meant by "we are one."

Fourteen years later, breath-based meditation is still my main form of meditation practice.

This discovery and feeling of "oneness and connection with the Divine" was a turning point in my spiritual journey and healing.

It led to a strong desire to share yoga and meditation with as many people as possible, especially in my then career as a probation officer working with young offenders and people serving custodial sentences.

Why Meditatoion Is Good for Your Health

People meditate for many reasons.

In my case, I first experienced meditation as a way to come to terms with the pain I felt after losing my brother (1997) and my cousin (1995) and the impact it was having on my ability to focus at work and care for my young family.

Similarly, most of my students turn to yoga and meditation when they are in some sort of personal and professional crisis.

They are stressed, overworked, and struggling with managing the complex demands of working in highly-pressurised careers.

Stress and burnout are on the rise and many employees and business owners *lose sleep and are anxious about the effect their work lives* have on their ability to be healthy and have meaningful relationships with their family and loved ones.

The relentless pace of life makes it hard for you to relax, spend quality time with your family, and get things done in a calm and considerate manner.

SEVEN COMMON SIGNS OF STRESS AND ITS DANGERS

1. You suffer unexplained aches and pains, maybe an old injury resurfaces, or you develop a backache. Nervous tension affects all muscles and joints. During your day, as pressure builds up, your body stiffens, and you experience headaches, back pain, neck pain, or indigestion.

2. You find it difficult to concentrate at work. Your inbox is full, and you dread going through your pile of work or checking your inbox because you are worried you may have missed something important.

3. You lack energy. You fret. You feel constantly tired and fatigued. Continuous worry drains you, and you are too worn out to do something physical, even though you know it will boost your energy.

4. You feel drained, frustrated, and even resentful by the demands placed on you. You may be caring for an elderly parent and raising a young child at the same time. You feel as if you don't have enough hands to do everything and find it difficult to express your feelings or ask for support.

5. Your heart beats faster and harder, which causes your pulse rate and blood pressure to rise. This can lead to heart failure and high blood pressure.

6. You can't slow down and have trouble switching off your brain. Your whole body is constantly in overdrive, and your mind is always racing. This leads to mental fatigue, eye strain, and in more serious cases, migraines and even memory loss.

7. No matter what you want to do, you don't have the energy to turn things around. You feel as if you are stuck in a rut.

STRESS KILLS. WHAT CAN YOU DO TO TURN YOUR LIFE AROUND?

What can you do to relax and de-stress, have more time for yourself and your family, or simply be more creative and alert at work?

When friends or loved ones ask, "How are you feeling?" do you grumble about how tough life is and gaze wistfully into the future, dreaming of your next vacation?

Wouldn't it be lovely if you could capture that happy, feel-good, vacation feeling anytime you wanted to?

Just imagine.

Whether it's Monday morning or you're doing-late night shopping on a Friday evening, in two minutes you are at your favourite holiday destination.

Just like that.

No bags to pack, no airport and check-in hassles, no lastminute panicking and searching for your passport or looking for someone to water your plants.

Wouldn't you like that?

To feel calm, happy, confident, cheerful, and relaxed?

The science and benefits of meditation are now clearly documented.

Meditation is the key to a stress-free life.

THE SCIENTIFIC BENEFITS OF MEDITATION

Science supports why you should meditate every day with research on the physical, emotional, and *mental* benefits.

And, a fascinating article at Mindvalley, "The Science Between Brainwaves and Meditation," demonstrates the correlation between meditation and the effects on your brainwaves.

In the *Forbes* article "7 Ways Meditation Can Actually Change The Brain," Alice G. Walton explores the research and studies conducted on the relationship between meditation and its effect on the brain.

Alice Walton cites evidence from numerous studies that highlight the positive effects of a regular meditation practice to preserve the ageing brain, reduce anxiety and social anxiety, and help with addiction.

The results confirm what ancient sages knew, that meditation relieves feelings of anxiety and depression and improves attention, concentration, and overall psychological well-being.

And if you are still a bit sceptical about how meditation can influence your mood, research by the David Lynch Foundation (**www.davidlynchfoundation.org.uk/research.html**) on the effects of meditation on your brain shows that transcendental meditation has many benefits to mind and body.

Meditation can:

Change the size of key regions of our brain

Improve our memory

Make us more empathetic and compassionate

Make us more resilient under stress

All pretty good stuff, eh?

As you can see, meditation has numerous benefits.

But based on conversations with students and friends, despite the scientific benefits of meditating, it appears that the actual *process* of meditating is fraught with challenges and obstacles that, in some cases, make it difficult for you to start meditation and stick with developing a daily habit. In the following chapter, we will look at the four most common obstacles most meditation beginners face when they meditate, and what you can do to overcome them.

Most Common Obstacles People Face

THE FOUR MOST COMMON OBSTACLES PEOPLE FACE WHILE MEDITATING ARE:

- Busy mind—your mind wanders off and you can't stop thinking
- Tiredness and falling asleep while you meditate
- Crazy-busy schedule so no time to meditate
- Finding a posture that works for you

OBSTACLE ONE: BUSY MIND

As a meditation teacher, I often hear statements like:

"I can never stop thinking."

"I have so many thoughts in my head. My mind is like a high-speed train rushing through a tunnel."

Or

"I have so many things to do. I feel overwhelmed and can't think clearly."

The stressful lives we lead and our growing dependence on technology (think of our attachment to our phones) negatively affects our ability to concentrate, focus, and relax.

But let me reassure you—that is *okay*.

That feeling of having a busy mind is perfectly normal.

Did you know that the average person has around 50,000 thoughts per day!

And considering there are 1400 minutes in a day that means (if my maths is correct!) we have at least 35 thoughts a minute!

No wonder you have a busy mind and struggle to stay focused!

Your mind is full of thoughts.

Coupled with this, 70% of these thoughts are believed to be negative! And the nature of the "monkey mind" makes it even harder for you to be still and meditate.

The ability to concentrate and keep your mind from wandering is perhaps one of the hardest aspects of meditation to overcome.

In meditation, you train your body to be still and your mind to slow down and focus on a point of concentration.

But some people struggle to sit still and prefer a more dynamic or active type of meditation, such as mindful walking meditation, which we will look at in the second part of this book.

Your mind has a mind of its own and has been likened to a chatting monkey.

When you sit to meditate, you realize just how busy your mind is. The whirlwind of cascading thoughts floating around makes it difficult to steady your thoughts, control your mind, and focus. Left untamed, your mind will jump from one topic or subject area to another.

This constant and habitual nature of the "jumping mind" or "monkey mind" is the main reason you find it so hard to focus and concentrate when you meditate.

SOLUTION: Practice easy yoga breathing exercises to calm your mind

The ancient art of yoga offers you many tools to help you relax your body, calm down, and steady your mind.

In fact, the original purpose of yoga was to prepare your mind and body to sit in meditation.

Yoga breathing exercises, known as Pranayama, are ideal practices to help you address your busy mind syndrome and help steady your mind.

In Chapter 7, The Best Way to Meditate, we will explore in more detail the role breathing exercises play in helping you meditate.

When you meditate, the purpose isn't to clear your mind of thoughts; rather, it is to allow your mind to stay focused on a point of concentration, for example, the breath.

When your mind wanders away from this point of concentration and you *notice* it has wandered and you then bring it back to your point of concentration—you are practicing meditation.

OBSTACLE TWO: TIREDNESS AND FALLING ASLEEP WHILE YOU MEDITATE

From experience, I know how easy it is to fall asleep while you meditate.

It is simple to do.

You sit down to meditate and because you are so tired, instead of sitting upright and meditating, you find yourself swaying, nodding off, and eventually falling asleep.

SOLUTION: Get more rest!

Sleep is your body's way to rest and repair.

If you find yourself drifting off while you meditate, accept what your body is telling you.

Go to bed and sleep.

You will wake up refreshed and in a better state to meditate.

If it isn't possible for you to sleep, maybe you are at work or have grabbed a few minutes out of the day to refresh, try doing a few rounds of yoga breathing exercises or practice simple yoga exercises.

If sleep is a problem for you, find a way to reschedule your routine so you get at least six to seven hours restful sleep every night.

Sleepytime is a brilliant app to help you select the best time you should sleep for maximum rest.

Lack of sleep is a vicious cycle.

The more you meditate, the more energy you will have—but if you are sleep deprived, you'll struggle to have the energy to meditate.

OBSTACLE THREE: CRAZY-BUSY AND NO TIME TO MEDITATE

Constantly rushing around and not having enough time to look after yourself so that you eventually burn-out is a popular reason many people start to meditate.

Trying to fit meditation into your already jam-packed day, especially if you have a busy family schedule and a demanding job, can seem impossible and feel like a nightmare.

You know caring for yourself is important, yet the competing demands you face from work and being there for your family and friends leave little time for you to relax and unwind.

Being too busy and lacking time to meditate has to be the biggest obstacle to practicing meditation.

Everyone is busy—trying to fit in yet another activity can seem like an insurmountable task.

Yet, as the Zen quote reminds us, the busier you are, the more you need to meditate.

Many celebrities, entrepreneurs, and top athletes swear that their daily meditation practice helps them to stay focused and have the energy to achieve all they do.

And you can do it too.

SOLUTION: Develop a routine

When you start meditation, it is easy to be enthusiastic and think you can meditate anytime anywhere. You can, but that level of expertise requires practice and time to develop.

It takes time and effort to find a gap in your schedule to meditate.

It is possible to press pause, take a few deep breaths, and practice self-love-on-the-go, yet deep calm and serenity come from making meditation a priority in your life and scheduling it into your day.

Be gentle and honest regarding your time availability. It is better to take a couple of days to look at your current schedule and determine how you can realistically set aside 5 to 15 minutes every day to meditate, than it is to try to squeeze in a manic 60-minute schedule "sometime" during the week.

You could aim to wake up 20 minutes earlier or switch off the TV 20 minutes earlier at night.

A good idea, and one that has worked well for me, is to find a meditation buddy. You don't have to meditate in the same place, but find someone who will agree to hold you accountable.

My friend and I used to take turns phoning each other every morning whilst we were setting up our meditation schedule.

As meditation buddies, we held each other accountable and shared our experiences and thoughts on our practice. I found it really helpful having that extra support and nudge to keep me going, especially in the winter when it is cold and dark when I wake up.

A couple years ago, a friend introduced me to the free meditation app, Insight Timer (**www.insighttimer.com**). This is a brilliant aid to help support your meditation practice as it offers a wide variety of guided meditations, meditation groups you can connect with, plus personal tracker and data analysis of your practice. I love it as it helps me stay accountable and I always get annoyed when I miss a day's practice and have to restart again from day 1!

OBSTACLE FOUR: POSTURE

When you meditate, it is important that you are comfortable.

Traditionally, sages sat on the floor in the lotus position and meditated. However, if you are like most of the people I work with, you struggle to sit still long enough to meditate.

Your body isn't used to sitting still, especially if you spend the lion's share of your day sitting, crouched over a computer with little time to rest or stretch your body.

Over time, this leads to a build-up of tension and fatigue in your lower back and hips and makes it uncomfortable for you to sit comfortably with a straight back in a crossed-legged position.

SOLUTION: Find a position that is comfortable for you.

It is *not* essential that you sit on the floor in full lotus position!

Your main priority is to ensure you are comfortable, that your mind is at ease, and that your spine is straight.

This allows energy to flow easily through your body.

For example, you can:

- Sit upright in a straight-backed chair
- Sit on the floor on a cushion with either your legs crossed or straight out in front of you
- Sit supported against a wall
- Lie down on the floor on your yoga mat/blanket or even lie on your back on your bed

(If you have lower back pain or feel uncomfortable lying on your back with your legs straight along the bed/mat, place your feet flat on the bed/mat, knees bent, and make sure your lower back is flat against the bed/mat.)

If you still struggle to sit still, another solution is to practice a more dynamic physical body-mind awareness meditation, such as walking meditation or even adult colouring.

3 | MOST COMMON OBSTACLES PEOPLE FACE

As with all new projects, practice makes perfect. If you wish to reap the benefits of meditation, you need to release your attachment to the desired outcome. Allow yourself to be present and focus on your chosen point of concentration. Rest when you are tired. And, ideally, practice at the same time every day.

I have covered four of the most common obstacles people face when they start to meditate, what have I missed?

If you struggle to relax and meditate, what obstacles get in *your way?* I would love to hear what you struggle with so that I can support you in overcoming your obstacles.

Drop me an email or leave me a review, and I'll get back to you.

So far, we have covered:

- What meditation is
- The health benefits gained from meditating
- The top four obstacles most people face while meditating

In the next chapter, we'll look at the five most common mistakes people make when they meditate and go over the seven-step process you need to follow to quickly meditate with ease.

Mistakes to Avoid When Meditating

FIVE MISTAKES TO AVOID MAKING WHEN MEDITATING

Although meditation is simple to learn, given the vast range of how-to-meditate books, audio programs, and online meditation programmes—for example, Live and Dare's five-week Meditation programme, *Master Your Mind*—it is easy to think that just by picking up a book on meditation, *or listening to a popular meditation podcast*, you will be a successful practitioner.

But as with all skills, you must learn the basics and practice these skills every day to reap the long-term benefits of meditation.

However, from teaching busy people to meditate and hearing their challenges, I've learned there are pitfalls and obstacles you need to avoid.

With support and a simple step-by-step method to follow, you can overcome these obstacles and easily learn how to relax and meditate.

The clearer you are about these "pitfalls," the easier it becomes for you to avoid making the following five common mistakes that will hinder your growth and efforts to meditate effectively.

#1 MEDITATION MISTAKE TO AVOID: YOU EXPECT INSTANT TRANSFORMATION

Great claims have been made about the power of meditation to transform your life.

As we touched on earlier, there are numerous studies showing that regular meditation practice reduces stress, calms your mind, and improves your concentration and focus at work.

The beauty of meditation is that you do feel a difference in energy when you meditate. You will feel calmer and relaxed. However, it takes weeks, sometimes even years, to achieve "total transformation." The reality is that the nature of the mind and the environment you live in mean that you have to constantly watch your thoughts and practice.

Change *can* happen overnight and most people do experience an immediate sense of calm when they meditate. Our stressful society and the roller-coaster effect it has on our emotions makes it hard to sustain that "positive vibe" once you finish your practice. So a lot of beginner students give up after only a few sessions because their problems still seem the same.

WHAT TO DO INSTEAD: If you've started to meditate but don't yet notice any difference in how you feel or respond in different situations, I strongly encourage you to stick with your practice.

Try another form of meditation and find a group of people who are also interested in learning how to meditate and want to make it part of their daily routine; this makes it easier for you to feel supported and stick with your practice.

When you commit to making meditation part of your daily schedule, you gradually change the grooves in your mind, and you *will* see results. Remember, Rome wasn't built in a day, and neither was a calm, peaceful mind and open heart. Trusting behavior takes skill and practice to achieve.

#2 MEDITATION MISTAKE TO AVOID: LACK OF REGULAR PRACTICE

I am sure you can remember one of your school teachers, or even your parents telling you that "practice makes perfect" every time you felt like giving up on something or found something too difficult to do. Alas, your mum and the school teacher were right!

To achieve anything in life you must practice. Meditation is no exception. To get any benefit from meditation you need to set time aside and practice.

WHAT TO DO INSTEAD: Little and often is the key. Make a commitment to practice at least 2–10 minutes every day rather than try and do a massive hour's practice once a month.

The four included guided meditations are ideal for busy beginners to learn the basics of meditation.

And for those of you who prefer more dynamic, active meditations, check out the seven meditations also included in the next section of this book.

#3 MEDITATION MISTAKE TO AVOID: BUILD-UP OF STRESS, FATIGUE, AND TENSION IN YOUR BODY

During the course of your day, you face many conflicting demands on your time, and it is easy to end up feeling stressed, overwhelmed, and exhausted. Most people ignore the early warning signs of stress and push their bodies to the limit and end up burnt out and demoralized. It is a vicious cycle. The more you push yourself to keep on top of work and family commitments, the more you expose yourself to stress-related illnesses. It becomes near impossible to rest, switch off your "brain," and give your body the rest and sleep it needs.

WHAT TO DO INSTEAD: Make self-care a priority and build regular "moments of calm" into your day.

Your mind and body are connected. Holding day-long tension in your body is dangerous to your long-term health and vitality. You must find a way to safely release pent-up frustration and anger. Having a daily morning self-care routine is vital to helping you start your day off in a positive and calm frame of mind.

Make a commitment to yourself to find ways during your day to take your foot off the pedal, to stretch, relax, and naturally calm your mind and energize your body.

Better still, share the article, 121 Employee Wellness Program Ideas Your Team Will Love (**www.snacknation.com/blog/employee-wellness-program-ideas**) with your team and managers, and choose a wellness activity your whole company can get involved in. Things like on-site yoga classes to relieve stress, walking meetings instead of sit-down meetings, and my favourite, keeping footballs, hula-hoops, and volleyballs around the office. How cool is that? Can you imagine your boss hula-hooping?!

#4 MEDITATION MISTAKE TO AVOID: LACK OF AWARENESS AND FOCUS DURING YOUR DAY

Closely related to MISTAKE #3, lack of awareness and focus during your day is counterproductive to your health and wellbeing. Meditation is not an isolated act, it is not something you do and then forget about until the next time you practice. Meditation is a skill, a technique you use to help you regain your focus and concentration any time during your day. Being present and aware of your posture, your thoughts, and your breath on a regular basis during your day are as vital as knowing your shoe size.

WHAT TO DO INSTEAD: Become more present during the day.

It is hard to do, yet the more you practice meditation and feel the difference it makes in your life, the more you will naturally become more aware and present of what is going on within and around you.

As a beginner, aim to develop a sense of mindfulness in your daily life.

For example, every now and then take a moment just to tune into your everyday breath and notice how you are breathing.

Whilst eating, rather than rushing through your meal and multi-tasking as you eat (texting, watching TV, speaking on the phone, working at your desk), pay attention to the tastes and sensations of the food as you eat.

Take a stretch break every hour or so to straighten your spine, relax your jaw, uncross your ankles and release tension in your body.

You can find more tips and yogic techniques to let go of stress in my popular *Yoga for Beginners Book* (**www.amazon.com/dp/B0767M437H**).

#5 MEDITATION MISTAKE TO AVOID: COMPARING YOUR EXPERIENCES WITH THOSE OF OTHERS

Meditation is a personal experience. The techniques and practices are universal, but how you feel and respond to these methods is as personal as your fingerprints. Every session you have is a unique experience, especially when you adopt the approach of a beginner's mind to your practice.

Many students make the mistake of comparing their experiences, thoughts, and impressions with those of other students. You may both be using the same techniques but their experience and yours may be totally different.

There is no right or wrong way to "feel" after meditating. For example, like me, you may have gone through a traumatic divorce, lost people close to you, or be going through a major organisational re-shuffle at work that keeps you up at night worrying about your job security. All these situations make it hard for you to settle into your practice and affect how you feel when you do. You might meditate and feel clear, calm, and confident, but another student may experience intense anger and sadness and burst out crying. This is okay, all perfectly normal, and all part of your meditation journey.

WHAT TO DO INSTEAD: Learn to adopt a nonjudgmental approach to your practice.

Meditation is your time-out with yourself. It isn't a house party, and there is no law saying how you must feel. Keep a journal and write down how you feel before and after each meditation session. Maintain a beginner's mind and, most importantly, connect with other like-minded people who can embrace, nourish, and support you during your practice and daily life.

Remember, meditation is like learning any new skill—riding a bike, learning to drive, baking a cake—you have to have patience, time, energy, and a supportive community to tap into to help you grow and develop your meditation muscle.

I encourage you to take your time and find a way to make meditation part of your life.

And, now that we have looked at the mistakes, obstacles, and benefits of meditating, let's put it all together and follow this simple seven-step guide to meditate with ease.

A Simple Guide to Meditate with Ease

FOLLOW THIS SIMPLE SEVEN-STEP GUIDE TO MEDITATE WITH EASE

Even if you hate to sit still, give this a go and see how you get on.

If you totally like it, check out the guided walking meditation and other forms of dynamic meditations listed below.

GENTLE REMINDER: If you haven't exercised for a while, or have a medical condition, please consult your doctor before starting any of the practices mentioned in this book.

Step 1: Find a Quiet Space and Set Your Intention

Step 2: Relax Your Body

Step 3: Calm Your Mind

Step 4: Check Your Posture

Step 5: Focus on Your Everyday Breath

Step 6: Breathe in and Breathe out for two to five minutes

Step 7: Smile and Enjoy the Moment

STEP 1: FIND A QUIET SPACE WHERE YOU CAN PRACTICE UNDISTURBED AND SET YOUR INTENTION

For many beginners, finding the "right place" to meditate is often the first hurdle you encounter. If your home and workspace are cluttered and full of noise and other people, it can be hard to find somewhere peaceful and quiet where you feel comfortable enough to meditate. Sometimes, going outside into nature and doing a walking meditation can be just as soothing as sitting down.

TIP: Be creative. Look outside your usual environment, maybe there is a quiet space or an empty office you can slip into during your lunch break. When my girls were little, I often sat at the top of the stairs, between household chores and my girls watching TV, to get five minutes of quiet time!

SET YOUR INTENTION

When you start to meditate, all kinds of thoughts, feelings, and sensations arise in your mind. Your mind will find all kinds of reasons for you not to meditate and because you are so used to always being on the go, being still and meditating can feel alien.

TIP: As you know, your thoughts determine the outcome of your behaviour. If you truly desire inner peace and relief from the busyness of your day, set your intention by quietly saying to yourself, "I am here to be still, calm, and clear my head."

STEP 2: RELAX YOUR BODY

If your body feels stiff and tense, do a few gentle yoga stretches. For example, wiggle your toes and make a few small circles with your feet; stretch your arms straight up above your head and lean to the left and then to the right. These movements will help release the build-up of muscular tension in your body making it easier for your body to relax and for you to sit still and be comfortable.

STEP 3: CALM YOUR MIND

Yoga breathing awareness exercises are the perfect way to calm your mind and settle your thoughts as you prepare to meditate.

Take a few minutes to hum quietly to yourself, or open your mouth wide and say "ahhhhhhhhhh" or "oooooooooooo" or even "eeeeeeeeeeeeeeeeeeeeeeee." This helps release stress and tension and gently trains your mind to refocus on your breath. In fact, if you are short on time, even just sitting quietly and repeating these three sounds for three to five cycles will help you feel calmer!

STEP 4: CHECK YOUR POSTURE

When you meditate, especially if practicing a seated form of meditation, you want your spine to be erect, your head, neck, and back in a straight line, aligned and relaxed, not tense and cramped up. You can sit on a chair, on the edge of your bed, the floor, or a meditation cushion. The key thing here is to be comfortable.

TIP: Take a few moments to become aware of how you are sitting.

If you are sitting on a chair, uncross your legs, make sure your feet are flat on the floor, toes pointing forwards. Rest your hands on your lap and take a soft gentle breath in and out through your nose. Lengthen your spine and lower your shoulders away from your ears. Check you aren't clenching your back teeth or locking your jaw and SMILE...that's the quickest way to release tension in your face!

STEP 5: FOCUS ON YOUR EVERYDAY BREATH

Turn your attention to your everyday breath, don't change the way you are breathing, but just start to notice. Observe and explore HOW you are breathing. For example, notice how long your in-breath is and how long your out-breath lasts; notice what happens to your belly and chest as you breathe in and out. Maybe notice the feeling of the out-breath on your upper lip, or even see if you can hear your breath.

TIP: Learning to become aware of how you are breathing, what happens to your body and even your mind as you breathe helps you turn your attention away from the everyday noise in your life and the chattering in your mind.

STEP 6: CONSCIOUSLY BREATHE IN AND BREATHE OUT FOR TWO TO FIVE MINUTES

Breathe in... Breathe out... Breathe in... Breathe out...

Stay focused on your breath as you gradually allow your everyday breath to go deeper and be longer. Stay in this state for two to five minutes and then sit quietly for a few more moments in quiet reflection before getting up and re-engaging with your day.

TIP: Sometimes it helps to set your phone timer for two to five minutes before you start the practice, close your eyes, and say a few positive words quietly to yourself as you breathe, which helps the mind focus and concentrate.

For example, once you have settled into being aware of your everyday breath, you can start to quietly say to yourself as you focus on your breath, "I breathe in... I breathe out" and coordinate the words with the movement of your breath."I breathe in (breathe in)... I breathe out (breathe out)... I breathe in... I breathe out... I breathe in... I breathe out..."

STEP 7: SMILE AND ENJOY THE MOMENT ☺

The Easiest Way to Meditate

WHAT'S THE EASIEST WAY TO MEDITATE?

I am often asked "What is the EASIEST way to learn how to meditate?

There is a common assumption that the only way to meditate is by sitting still in a classic meditation pose.

However, as you'll see in the meditation techniques below, there are other ways to experience the benefits without having a seated practice.

That said, based on personal preference and feedback from students, I would say focusing on your breath, whether doing a seated or more active meditation, is key to having a successful meditation practice.

In this chapter, we'll have a look at the role the breath plays in healthy living, how to breathe, benefits of healthy breathing, and how to use your breath as a guide in meditation.

We'll start with a general introduction into the benefits of good breathing and how meditation helps you breathe better.

THE BENEFITS OF GOOD BREATHING HABITS TO HELP YOU MEDITATE

So let's discover how you can use your breath to:

- Quickly calm your mind and body to bring you back into balance.
- Relieve anxiety, worry, and frustration so that you increase your ability to focus and concentrate at work when the pressure is on.

What happens when you breathe correctly?

On a basic level, breathing in allows you to draw oxygen into your body, and breathing out eliminates toxins and bacteria that impede your body's ability to function properly.

The slower and deeper you can breathe, the more you allow oxygen to enter and flow through your body. This expands your lung capacity, stimulates and opens your heart, which instantly makes you feel more confident, brighter, and happier.

THREE BENEFITS OF GOOD BREATHING HABITS

1. Enhances your emotional and physical well-being so you feel healthier and calmer
2. Releases tension and pressure on your heart which reduces risk of heart-related medical conditions
3. Triggers the parasympathetic nervous system which promotes rest and relaxes and rejuvenates your body and calms your mind

DO YOU KNOW THE POWER OF YOUR BREATH?

Learning how to breathe correctly is one of the most important lessons you will learn when you start to meditate.

From a yogic perspective, your breath is the link between your mind and your body.

Learning to breathe well is a skill. You may be surprised to realize that your breath is directly linked to your body. Understanding the link between the mind and body connection enables you to look at ways you can improve your health.

When you breathe deeply and fully you activate the parasympathetic branch of the central nervous system. This system allows the "rest and digest" response to filter through your body—as opposed to the "fight and flight" stress response of the sympathetic nervous system that generally governs your life.

WHAT ARE YOGA BREATHING EXERCISES?

Traditionally, yoga breathing exercises form the core of yoga. Known as pranayama, (control of the breath), deep breathing exercises provide you with an easy way to ease tension and restore energy and vitality anytime you need it.

WHAT HAPPENS TO YOUR BREATH WHEN YOU ARE UPSET AND ANGRY?

Have you noticed that when you are tense your breath is fast and shallow? Or maybe you hold your breath when anxious.

Conversely, when you are angry your breathing is rapid and sharp, or when you are depressed and sad your breath is uneven and slightly jumpy. However, when you are relaxed, happy, and joyful your breath is slow and even. This is the ideal way to breathe.

WHY IS YOGA BREATHING SO IMPORTANT?

Learning how to breathe correctly can help you manage the negative effects of stress as headaches, stomach disorders, fatigue, sleepless nights, and anxiety at work.

Everyone suffers from nervous tension and anxiety at some time in their life. You may be going through a painful divorce or mourning the loss of a close relative or family friend. You might be facing disciplinary procedures at work or recovering from major surgery. All these incidents affect your immune system, which in turn can lower your ability to stay vital and on top of things.

WHAT HAPPENS TO YOUR BODY WHEN YOU BREATHE CORRECTLY?

If you look around your workplace or when out travelling on public transport, you will notice that many people do not breathe fully. They are short of breath, or breathe heavily, taking gasping breaths when they speak, or constantly yawning to try to draw fresh oxygen into their bodies. Learning to understand your particular breathing habits is an important step in helping you gauge what is happening on a mental, emotional, and physical level.

When you breathe in through your nose, you draw oxygen into your body. Your heart pumps oxygenated blood all around your body. A gaseous exchange takes place whereby your cells receive oxygen and release carbon dioxide (a waste product) that is carried back to your lungs and finally exhaled.

The slower and deeper you breathe, the more you allow oxygen to enter and flow through your system. This expands your lung capacity, stimulates and opens up your heart, and instantly revitalizes and energizes your body. All of which enhances your ability to manage the demands of your busy work and home be in a calm and more productive way.

Paying attention and being aware of how you breathe is the easiest way to master the art of meditation. When you practice the breathing awareness exercises found in Section Two, you'll instantly feel calmer and clearer.

The beauty of meditation is that it is an ongoing, unfolding personal development process that enables you to become more aware of your emotional states, thoughts, feelings, and actions and identify those that are healthy and unhealthy and ultimately lift or zap your energy. There are so many distractions in your daily life that taking the time to pause and consciously breathe is a gift you can give yourself—and in so doing give to others who will feel your sense of calm and inner confidence.

Quick & Easy Ways to Meditate

SEVEN QUICK AND EASY WAYS TO HAVE THE BEST MEDITATION EVER

I want to congratulate you for staying the course and taking steps to learn easy and effective way to relax, reduce stress, and meditate. The meditation techniques and breathing awareness exercises in the next section offer you a chance to put into practice some of what you have read.

I do hope you find them useful in supporting your desire for less stress and more energy to do the things that matter most to you.

Before going to the meditations, I'd like to offer you a final tip on how to meditate better and keep up your practice.

In the heat of the moment, it is easy to lose sight of your "Why?" and fall prey to the common obstacles and mistakes most people make when learning how to meditate.

I want you to succeed and be happy and healthy. That's why in this final section I've included seven super simple tips to help you meditate. These tips will give you another layer of support in keeping up your meditation practice.

#1 BEST EVER MEDITATION TIP—KEEP IT REAL

Life is busy and there will be days, weeks, maybe even months when you don't practice. That's okay. That's life. You will wake up one day and you will sit and practice.

#2 BEST EVER MEDITATION TIP—BE LOVING

Meditation is a gift you give yourself. And as with all gifts, take your time to enjoy the feeling of anticipation and excitement as you unwrap your present.

#3 BEST EVER MEDITATION TIP—BREATHE

This is the key to your practice. Anytime, anywhere you feel off key and your mind is on overdrive and cluttered…just breathe. Slowly. Gently. With presence and conscious awareness. Breathe and you will soon feel better.

#4 BEST EVER MEDITATION TIP—BE CREATIVE

As you can see from the meditation exercises and breathing awareness exercises, there are many ways to learn how to meditate. Take your pick. The more you practice, the deeper and more confident you become in "knowing" what technique you need to use to regain your calm, let go of stress, and relax your body and mind.

#5 BEST EVER MEDITATION TIP—SMILE

#6 BEST EVER MEDITATION TIP— ASK FOR SUPPORT

There is an old saying in yoga: *When the student is ready, the teacher will appear.*

Anytime you feel stuck, unsure, or need a helping hand to get you by, just breathe and in the quiet of your heart say a prayer and ask for help, for guidance, clarity, and the confidence to know that what you seek will be provided.

#7 BEST EVER MEDITATION TIP— TRUST

At the end of the day, meditation is a state of mind. The practice of meditation is just a tool to guide you to feel calm, inner peace, and balance in your everyday life.

Special Bonus Section

Before we get into the bonuses, let's review what we have covered so far. We have looked at the health benefits gained from meditation and noted the signs and effects of stress on the body. We covered the most common mistakes and obstacles and you practiced a simple seven-step framework to help you meditate.

Everything leading up to this point has focused on helping you feel comfortable to meditate.

It's time now to put all this theory into practice and try your hand at practicing a variety of other meditations. In this section, we'll introduce you to:

- Four breath-based meditations for beginners.
- Three yoga breathing exercises.
- Two breathing exercises you can practice with your children.
- And eight non-seated/dynamic meditations.

The Special Bonus Meditation for Beginners Guided Meditations and Yoga Breathing Exercises are super simple to do. You can practice anywhere, anytime you feel stressed-out, fatigued, or anxious. You'll feel better straight away as you calm and clear your mind and relax tension from your body.

Let's begin!

Four easy breath-based meditations and three yoga breathing awareness exercises to help you meditate with ease.

GENTLE REMINDER: As with all mind-body exercises, please respect and listen to your body. Move with grace, and appreciate the wonders of your breath.

GUIDED MEDITATION #1: EASE TENSION AND CALM YOUR MIND

Set your intention and quietly say to yourself the following affirmation: "I give thanks for my health and the joys of living and being alive." Or, if you prefer, you can say your favourite inspirational verse.

- Sit in a comfortable position and give yourself permission to relax and unwind for two to ten minutes.
- Turn your attention to your breath and listen to the sound and movement of your everyday breath flowing softly in and out through your nose (if you wish you can close your eyes).
- On your next breath, slowly breathe in and quietly count "one."
- Breathe out and count "two."
- Breathe in and count "three."
- Breathe out and count "four."
- Continue counting your breaths up to ten.
- When you reach number ten, go back to number one and repeat the practice for two to ten minutes.
- If your mind wanders during the practice and you lose concentration, that's okay. Just return your attention back to your breath and begin counting from number one.
- And when you are ready, if your eyes are closed, slowly open your eyes and notice what has changed about your mind's state and the energy of your thoughts.

GUIDED MEDITATION #2: BREATHING AWARENESS EXERCISES TO EASE YOU INTO YOUR DAY

I breathe, relax, stand tall and proud because I am proud of who I am.

This guided breathing awareness exercise is ideal to do first thing in the morning before you engage in your daily activities. It will help instil a sense of purposeful calm and focus as you prepare for your day.

- Take a moment right now to check on your posture.
- How are you sitting or standing?
- Take a gentle breath in through your nose and as you breathe out, tune in to see what is going on in your mind, what thoughts, feelings, and emotions are there bubbling under the surface?
- Exhale and relax your jaw, lower your shoulders, lift your chest up, feel your spine lengthening as you allow your neck to float up and be long; smile with your eyes and appreciate how graceful and poised you look; remember you are a pure soul, a divine being walking this Earth.
- Turn your attention to your breath and start to notice how you are breathing.
- Let your breath be soft and gentle; don't change the way you are breathing, just observe the way your breath flows in, around, and through your body.
- Keep your jaw relaxed; slowly open your mouth and silently whisper the word AAAAHHHHH…as you breathe out. See how long you can keep going whispering AAAHHHH before you naturally start to breathe in; and on your next exhale, open your mouth a bit wider and quietly say aloud another round of AAAHHHHHHs. Repeat this three to five times and each time, allow your AAAHHHHH sound to be longer and go deeper and deeper into your body.
- If you wish you can close your eyes as you meditate.
- After you have done three to five rounds, remain still for a few more moments, noticing what has changed about the way you feel and observe the sensations and impressions flowing through your body and mind.

GUIDED MEDITATION #3: REDUCE FATIGUE, FRUSTRATION, AND FEEL BETTER SO EVERY DAY IS A NEW DAY

Be gentle and allow your practice to unfold with grace and ease.

If you are having one of those days, I invite you to practice the following Just Be Meditation. It is quick and easy to do and a simple technique you can slip in anywhere anytime you feel frustrated, anxious, or overwhelmed. The practice can be done in as little as two minutes, and you'll instantly feel refreshed, rebalanced, and able to give your full attention to the task at hand.

JUST BE...

Find a comfortable seat, make yourself as comfortable as you can and gently take a long steady breath out through your nose. On the next in-breath start to observe the way your belly rises and falls as you breathe in and out.

NEXT...

- Turn your attention to your thoughts and start to observe and notice the thoughts, feelings, and emotions flowing through your mind.
- Don't judge them, just notice what you notice as if you are gazing up at the sky and watching the clouds drift by.
- Allow your thoughts to flow naturally and see them for what they are—just thoughts... Can you name and label the thoughts, or who the thought is directed to?
- Every time you become aware of your thoughts, consciously turn your attention back to your breath and listen to the sound and movement of your breath as you inhale...exhale...inhale...exhale...stay with this process for five to ten more minutes, alternating your awareness between your breath, your thoughts, and the sounds you can hear.
- And when you are ready, slowly bring the practice to a close by returning your attention to the sounds you can hear in the room you are in and slowly continue with your day.
- Sometimes, it just takes a few minutes of turning your attention to your breath to release tension and bring yourself back into a centre of calm, tranquillity, and inner peace.

GUIDED MEDITATION # 4: FOR INNER PEACE, HAPPINESS, AND CALM

I trust everything and anything I require for health, growth, and healing is already provided.

Although this meditation is designed to be practiced in bed as you wake up, you can practice it anytime during the day when you feel pushed, strained, or pulled in too many directions.

It is easy to do, and within two minutes you instantly feel refreshed and rebalanced. Practiced first thing in the morning, it also helps you set your intention for the day and affirms your sense of self love.

Lying on your back on your bed, make sure you feel comfortable and your back is supported. If you suffer from lower back pain, this can be eased by having your legs resting straight out along the bed and placing a firm pillow underneath your knees, or you can rest the soles of your feet on your bed, knees up.

Place your right hand on your upper chest and your left hand on your lower abdomen.

Spend a few moments listening to all the sounds you can hear in the room. Maybe a clock ticking or the central heating boiler burping. If it is raining or windy, turn your attention to the sounds the elements make when they touch other surfaces.

Gradually, turn your attention to your hands (still resting on your chest and belly) and take a slow steady breath in through your nose for a count of one-two-three-four. Then slowly exhale through your nose one-two-three-four.

Repeat this five to seven times.

In your mind's eye, start to imagine you are standing in front of an open doorway looking out onto a stunning landscape.

With each breath, keep "looking" at the view, feel the splendour and majestic beauty of the landscape filling you up.

With each breath say to yourself "I am peace" as you hold the scene before you in your mind's eye.

Repeat the affirmation, "I am peace," five to seven times, and when you are ready, bring your attention back to your hands resting on your chest and belly.

Spend a few more moments listening to the sounds you can hear in and around your room. Gradually open your eyes and return your hands back to your side.

THREE BREATHING AWARENESS EXERCISES TO HELP YOU MEDITATE WITH EASE

ANYWHERE, ANYTIME, YOGA BREATHING EXERCISES TO BEAT STRESS, FATIGUE AND RESTORE ENERGY

Learning how to relax, recognize, and manage your stress levels is essential to helping you stay healthy and happy.

Some people find meditation challenging to do because their thoughts run rampant, and they struggle to focus their attention on their breath.

In this situation, I suggest you focus on practicing yoga breathing exercises as a way to train your mind to concentrate.

Yoga breathing exercises offer you a quick tool to release tension, reduce the effects of stress on your body, and calm your mind. They are useful strategies to employ to support your intention to be healthy and happy.

The first yoga breathing exercise, Diaphragmatic Breathing, is a foundational breathing exercise I encourage yoga and meditation students to practice.

Most of my students say it gives them the maximum benefit in releasing pressures. It is simple to do and can be practiced anywhere and at any time of the day when you feel drained yet need to focus, stay alert, and get stuff done.

When you practice yoga breathing exercises, remember to relax your shoulders, and lightly tuck your chin in. This helps keep your head, neck, and back in a nice straight line.

DIAPHRAGMATIC BREATHING

You can practice diaphragmatic breathing while lying on your back on a comfortable surface, for example your bed, or sitting comfortably in a chair, or even standing up.

BENEFITS: Helps to develop concentration and balances the right and left sides of the brain.

- Gently place one hand on your upper chest and the other hand on your belly.
- Relax your belly and chest.
- Keep your mouth closed.
- Breathe in through your nose and feel your belly rising and expanding, then feel your ribcage rising and, finally, your upper chest.
- As you exhale, feel your belly sink down. If you wish to close your eyes to help you concentrate, that is fine.
- Practice five to seven rounds of diaphragmatic breathing, then slowly open your eyes.
- Be still for a few moments until you feel ready to gently re-engage with your day.

The following two yoga breathing exercises, Single Nostril Breathing and Alternate Nostril Breathing, are slightly more advanced yoga breathing exercises, so I'd suggest you practice them only after you feel confident and comfortable practicing diaphragmatic breathing, and ideally under the guidance of a yoga/meditation teacher.

Regular practice of Single Nostril Breathing and Alternate Nostril Breathing will encourage full, deep breathing. With regular practice, this will help calm your mind and be an excellent preparation for meditation.

SINGLE NOSTRIL BREATHING EXERCISE FOR DEEP CALM

BENEFITS: A calming breathing practice, Single Nostril Breathing helps create balance in the body.

Breathing through your right nostril helps to stimulate your energy, while breathing through your left nostril calms and relaxes your emotions.

To get the most out of this breathing exercise, practice Part A (breathing through your right nostril) in the morning and Part B (breathing through your left nostril) in the evening before you go to sleep.

PART A: Sit in a comfortable position, spine straight, body relaxed.

- Rest your left hand on your lap.
- Turn your attention to your right hand. Bend your index and middle fingers into your palm. Your thumb, ring, and little finger are up (this position is known as *Vishnu Mudra*).
- Your thumb is used to close your right nostril, and your ring and little finger your left nostril.
- Close your left nostril with your ring and little fingers.
- Breathe in through your right nostril for a count of four, and then slowly breathe out for a count of eight.
- Repeat this five to ten times.
- Relax and return your right hand to your lap.

PART B: In the evening, just before you go to bed, repeat the above steps, but this time:

- Close your right nostril, using your right thumb.
- Breathe in through your left nostril for a count of four, and then slowly breathe out for a count of eight.
- Repeat this five to ten times.
- Relax and return your hands to your lap. Take a few moments to sit still and notice how you feel.

ALTERNATE NOSTRIL BREATHING

WHAT IS ALTERNATE NOSTRIL BREATHING?

Alternate Nostril Breathing (traditionally known as Anuloma Viloma) is a classic yogic breathing exercise and practiced at the beginning or end of a yoga session and is an ideal preparation for meditation.

WHEN DO YOU PRACTICE ALTERNATE NOSTRIL BREATHING?

Whenever you feel out of alignment and start getting ratty and tense or feel anxious—that's a sign your energy needs to be re-aligned and rebalanced.

Alternate Nostril Breathing helps with this process because it alternates the flow of breath (prana) through one nostril and then the other.

HOW DO YOU PRACTICE ALTERNATE NOSTRIL BREATHING?

As with all yoga exercises, please listen and respect your body. Any sign of discomfort, dizziness, or pain in the body, please stop, rest, and if needed, see your doctor. If you are pregnant or new to yoga, I suggest you familiarize yourself with more basic yoga breathing exercises before trying this more advanced practice.

SIMPLE GUIDELINES FOR THE PRACTICE OF ALTERNATE NOSTRIL BREATHING

Traditionally, Alternate Nostril Breathing is practiced in the ratio of 1:4:2. That is, for every second/count of breath you inhale, you retain your breath for four times as long and then exhale for twice as long.

For example, if you inhale for a count of 2, then you hold your breath for a count of 8, and exhale for account of 4.

Once you feel comfortable with this ratio, slowly start to lengthen your practice, and inhale for a count of 4, retain for a count of 16, and breathe out for a count of 8. There are six core steps to complete one round of Alternate Nostril Breathing

Before you start, make sure you are sitting comfortably either on a chair or cross-legged on the floor. Spend a few moments in quiet contemplation focusing on your everyday breath as you invite your mind and body to settle into the practice.

Sit upright with a straight spine.

Rest the back of your left hand on your left knee, with your thumb and index finger touching.

With your right hand, bend your index and middle fingers into your palm, which leaves your right thumb to close your right nostril and your ring and little fingers to close your left nostril.

STEP 1: Close your right nostril with your right thumb and slowly exhale fully through your left nostril for a count of four.

STEP 2: Gently hold your breath by pinching both nostrils between your thumb and ring and little fingers for a count of 16.

STEP 3: Release your thumb from your right nostril (keep your left nostril closed) and exhale through your right nostril for a count of eight.

STEP 4: Keeping your left nostril closed, breathe in through your right nostril for a count of four.

STEP 5: Close both nostrils and hold your breath for a count of 16 (as in #2).

STEP 6: Release your left fingers from your left nostril, keep your right nostril closed with your right thumb and breathe out through the left nostril for a count of eight.

This completes one round of this practice. Aim to do between three and seven rounds.

SPECIAL BREATHING EXERCISE FOR CHILDREN—THE BUMBLE BEE BREATH AND THE LION ROAR!

The following two breathing exercises for children are fun to do with your child, especially if they love making loud animal noises—you can even do them by yourself if you don't mind making loud animal sounds!

#1 BREATHING EXERCISE FOR CHILDREN: THE BUMBLE BEE BREATH

Make sure your child is sitting comfortably with their back straight.

Ask your child to close their eyes and slowly breathe in through their nose, and then ask them to pretend they are a bumble bee and to make a long humming sound as they breathe out.

They can make a high humming sound one time and a low or soft and gentle humming sound the next.

Repeat this humming pattern three to seven times.

For the last breath, encourage your child not to make any sound at all and to listen to the silence and notice what has changed about how they feel.

YOGA PARENTING TIP: Practice the Bumble Bee breathing exercise with your child.

Make it a fun game, see who can buzzzz the longest and then enjoy the silence together at the end of the exercise.

#2 BREATHING EXERCISE FOR CHILDREN: THE LION ROAR

The Lion Roar is one of my yoga students' (young and old) favourite breathing exercises because it is fun to do and quickly helps you release frustration and the build-up of anxiety and stress.

BENEFITS: Fun to do and helps your child understand the power of their breathing to calm, balance, and quiet their thoughts.

- Sit or stand comfortably.
- Scrunch up your face like a dried prune.
- Open your eyes and look upward.
- Open your mouth, stretch out your tongue, and *roarrrrrr* like a lion. Repeat three times and when you've finished, smile and notice how you feel. I guarantee you'll feel better.

YOGA PARENTING TIP: Children love this breathing exercise.

If your child is bored or grumpy and miserable, get them up and do the Lion Roar.

The longer and louder they roar, the more frustration they'll release and that will make them feel calmer and happier.

MEDITATION EXERCISES FOR PEOPLE WHO CAN'T SIT STILL

At the beginning of this book I said we would also include meditation techniques and breathing exercises for people who want to meditate but hate to sit still.

Some people find it easier to meditate if they are physically doing an activity and engaging their body in their practice.

If this sounds like you, or you just want to try a different meditation technique, the following techniques are ideal for you and can be practiced in addition to the above seated meditation techniques, breathing exercises, or by themselves as stand-alone meditation exercises.

Whether you practice a seated meditation or a more dynamic form (see below), the key things to remember are:

- Keep your attention focused on your point of concentration
- Stay aware of your breath
- Breathe deeply throughout your dynamic practice
- Keep your attention focused on your chosen activity

In fact, most of the dynamic, active types of meditation work best when you "lead with your breath" and move with your breath.

6 DYNAMIC/ACTIVE MEDITATION TECHNIQUES FOR PEOPLE WHO HATE TO SIT STILL

1. Mindful walking
2. Mindful eating and eating in silence
3. Mindful knitting or craft work
4. Writing meditation
5. Being in nature meditation
6. Adult colouring Mandala meditation

#1 MINDFUL GUIDED WALKING MEDITATION

WALKING MEDITATION

Guided walking meditation is the most popular form of dynamic/active meditation most beginners try. So, I'll go into a bit more detail here about walking meditation to give you an overview of this type of meditation.

You can do a simple walking meditation in as little as two minutes in your bedroom, kitchen, office space, in fact anywhere where you have space to walk in a circle or in a straight line for a few steps!

WHAT IS A GUIDED WALKING MEDITATION?

Simply put, a walking meditation is a way of walking whereby you bring your attention inwards and pay attention to and embrace all the sensations you notice in your body as you walk. It's a beautiful practice and, as with all meditation techniques, the more you practice it, the easier it becomes for you to experience a shift in your energy.

BENEFITS: Walking meditation helps ground your energy. If you spend a lot of time "in your head" worrying, anxious, and frightened about a situation, a walking meditation is a great way to clear and calm your thoughts. As you pay attention to the experience of walking, the process helps to stabilise and balance your energy and brings a sense of calm and peace to your body.

HOW TO WALK AND CALM YOUR MIND

Find a quiet space where you can walk outside, ideally barefoot, in a park or on the beach, undisturbed for two to five minutes. If this isn't possible, then you can practice indoors. If walking indoors, make sure the area is clear of clutter and you can walk in a circle or take a few steps in a straight line and turn back again.

Stand in a comfortable position and take a moment to observe your everyday breath. Gradually allow your breath to soften and deepen.

Start to turn your attention to your posture and notice what you notice about the way you are standing; bring your awareness to the sensations and impressions you are aware of within your body. Stay focused on your breath as you continue to tune in to your body.

Wiggle your toes and spread them evenly back onto the floor.

Bring your attention to your eyes. Have a soft downward gaze and focus on a point about two feet in front of your feet. Keep this soft focus throughout the practice.

Take three more gentle steadying breaths…inhale…exhale…inhale…exhale…inhale…exhale.

Start to walk following this pattern:

Breathe in and lift your right foot.

Breathe out and step your right foot forward a few inches and place it back on the ground.

Slight pause as you observe what is happening within your body.

Breathe in and lift your left foot.

Breathe out and step your left foot forward and place it back on the ground.

Repeat this pattern of coordinating the in-breath with the lifting of one foot and the out-breath with placing it back on the ground for two to five minutes or for as long as you feel comfortable. Work to your own rhythm and enjoy the sensations and messages flowing from your body as you attentively walk for the duration of your practice.

TIPS: As you walk, it is useful to pay attention to the following points:

Sense the movement taking place in your body.

Notice the way your ankles, knees, thighs, hips, and shoulders bend and straighten and move with each step and breath you take.

Observe the alignment of your head, neck, and back as you walk. Don't judge what you notice, just maintain a sense of open curiosity and wonder at your body as you coordinate each step with your breath.

What thoughts, feelings, and sensations are you aware of as you walk?

How do you feel walking slowly and with awareness?

How often during your day do you pay attention to the way you walk and the effect it has on your breath and posture?

If your mind wanders away from your body and you become aware of other thoughts, gently guide your focus back to coordinating each action of the walking process with your breath.

Practice as long as you feel comfortable, and gradually come to a stationary position. Pause for a few moments noticing what you notice and when you are ready, gracefully re-engage with your day.

#2 TWO MINDFUL EATING MEDITATIONS

1. EATING IN SILENCE PRACTICE

I first encountered "mindful eating meditation" whilst going through a 12-month personal and spiritual development programme in 2000. We had a group lunch and had to eat in silence and "pay attention" to what and how we ate. The first time I tried this, I freaked out because I always associate mealtimes as a place to chat and converse with others.

But the more mindful silent meals we had, the deeper I connected with my food and the others in my group. We developed ways to communicate without speaking. We tuned in to each other's body language and noticed when someone silently wished for a dish to be passed or needed a refill for their drink. It is an incredible experience.

And if your mealtimes are like most people in that you allow mobile gadgets to be part of your mealtime, then eating mindfully is an opportunity to bring that sense of calm and silence into your mealtime.

Another way you can practice mindful eating is by having an eating meditation practice.

2. MINDFUL EATING MEDITATION PRACTICE

In this meditation, you are still sitting, but your focus is on the food you are eating. It is a very sensory process and you take time and effort to really savour and indulge your senses in your food. Most of the time, we eat in a very auto-pilot, grab and eat-on-the-go way. Practicing mindful eating is a wonderful way to bring the essence of meditation into your daily life.

Here's a quick how to....

Chose a plate and lovingly place three slices of three different fruits on it.

Choose fruits or a spoonful of foods you like and some you don't like of different textures and flavours, maybe a slice of lemon, a grape, and a strawberry. (Traditionally this exercise is done with a raisin, but it is nice to experiment and explore the practice with a range of fruit.)

Before you start to eat, take a moment to centre yourself, take three deep breaths and allow your body to relax.

Turn off distractions, like the radio or TV or mobiles, and turn your full attention to the plate of fruit/food before you.

Notice the way the fruit is resting on the plate, the shape of each fruit, and the space they take up. Really use your eyes to distinguish the shades and hues of the individual slices.

Then, notice your hands and the way your hand and body move towards the fruit.

Observe any sensations or thoughts going through your mind while you decide which fruit/food to pick up first. Is it your favourite one? Don't judge or analyse what and why, just observe and notice how you pick up the fruit, the way it feels in your fingers, its texture and size. Does it feel rough? Smooth? Squishy?

Do you notice the different fruit smells? And how about your taste buds, are you salivating at the thought of tasting the fruit, or maybe you sense your face tense as you pick up a fruit you aren't familiar with or don't like. Again, just observe and notice how you respond to this movement.

As you bring the fruit towards your mouth, again notice how you are holding the fruit. How firm is your grip? Are you holding it with your fingers or scooped up and resting in your palm.

Again, just bring that sense of curiosity and openness to how you are holding the fruit. Do you bring the fruit to your mouth or do you lean over and bring your body down to meet the fruit? Notice what you notice.

What is going on as the fruit enters your mouth? Do you want to eat the whole slice in one gulp or can you resist that urge and take a small bite and notice how long you chew? Really chew the fruit. How does that feel? What thoughts are going through your mind as the fruit enters through your mouth and begins to slide down your throat and into your stomach?

Again, take your time and notice all that is going on within your mind and body and how you're breathing as you mindfully repeat this exercise with the other slices of fruit.

#3 MINDFUL KNITTING OR CRAFT WORK

My daughters love to knit and crochet. For them, this is their preferred way of meditating, of being still, of turning their attention in and focusing their minds. Each stitch is carefully crafted and slipped over their fingers and onto the needle. They do shift their posture and move, but generally when they are knitting, they are very much in the moment and at the end of their knitting/crochet time they have created a work of art and something they are proud of.

Give it a go. If you are interested in exploring this form of active meditation, you can even go on a Mindful Knitting Retreat (**www.twinwillows.ca/mknittingretreat**) as a way to go deeper into your practice.

#4 WRITING MEDITATION

As a writer, writing meditation is one of my favourite forms of meditation, especially on the days when my mind is on overdrive and I find it hard to sit still. Holding a pen and consciously bringing my attention to what I'm writing helps slow down my thoughts.

Here's how to do it.

Find your quiet space and bring with you a journal or sheet of paper and a pen.

You can also bring an inspirational poem or prayer with you.

Make yourself comfortable. Take a few deep breaths and when you are ready, pick up your pen.

You can slowly and deliberately copy out your inspirational poem or prayer, writing in tune with your breath and paying attention to how you feel. Or, you can choose a special symbolic word, such as "peace" or "truth" and write out the word, slowly and mindfully, at least 50 times, taking time to meditate and ponder on the way your hand and pen connect and glide across the page.

After you have completed your sacred meditative writing, stay still for a while longer before re-engaging with your everyday life.

#5 BEING IN NATURE STARING UP AT THE SKY

Staring up at the sky is a simple meditation technique you can do anywhere anytime you want a fresh perspective on life, especially if you love being outdoors and feel cramped and stifled when stuck indoors!

Take a moment to step outside and find a quiet space where you can stand. If it's too cold to go outdoors, you can practice this meditation by staying inside and looking through a window. Or, if you're stuck on a busy tube, you can hold onto a handrail, close your eyes, and visualise and practice this meditation.

Take a few moments to reconnect with your breath, and when ready, gaze up at the sky.

Observe the colours, textures of the clouds, or if it's night, look for the stars and moon.

Take a few steady breaths as you lower your shoulders, stretch out your fingers and toes, and start to ease any tension or stress from your body.

Stay focused on the feeling of relaxation in your body as you continue to notice how you are breathing. Gaze around and observe the vastness of the sky. If you wish, stretch up your arms (think of Rafiki in *The Lion King* presenting Simba to the pride).

Allow yourself to bask in the spaciousness and awe of the moment and recognise that you too are part of this great expansive creation we call the Earth. Each breath you take in, feel as if you are absorbing the magic and splendour of the Earth. And as you breathe out, allow your body to relax a bit more as you tune in and rest in the silence and spaciousness inside your mind.

Stay in this space, taking five to ten slow, steady, refreshing breaths before returning to your everyday breath and surroundings.

#6 COLOURING MANDALA MEDITATION

Similar to writing meditation and even mindful eating, colouring mandala meditation practice is another form of meditation you can use if you hate to sit still.

Mandala is the Sanskrit word for circle. Many mandalas have spiritual or religious meanings and were originally associated with ancient religions. A mandala shows that life is never ending and represents our connectedness with each other and the universe.

Nowadays, mandalas are commonly used as images that you colour in. They come in a variety of geometric shapes and are often connected with random circular images from nature.

Colouring in mandalas is seen as a form of active, open meditation because your focus is on the shapes and colours and images you are colouring in. Mindful colouring in your mandala allows your mind to settle and your body to relax and helps you start to "tune in" to your creative space.

When I teach yoga to children, as a way to encourage them to relax and refocus their energy, I like to end the sessions with a short mandala meditation colouring practice. Often, even the most active and fidgety child is soon absorbed and engaged in choosing their colouring pencils and gaily colouring in their mandalas. Colouring in mandalas is another way to turn your thoughts inwards and allow your inner beauty and creativity to shine. Even people who do not see themselves as "artistic" find a rhythm and breath as they colour in their mandalas.

Conclusion

So, if you hate to sit still, yet desire to live a calm and peaceful life, the guided meditations, breathing exercises, and dynamic meditations included in this book will serve you well.

ALL THE TIPS and suggestions in this book are activities my clients and I practice to help us reduce stress, relax, and have energy to do the things that matter most to us.

I have shared the seated and more dynamic meditation techniques here to inspire and encourage you to take time out of your daily schedule to take care of *you*.

I want you to feel relaxed and know how to soothe away stress and find calm, especially when you have to juggle the demands of running a busy household, caring for your family, and keeping on top of matters at work.

I hope you found the meditations in this book useful, especially the meditations offered for people who hate to sit still. Let me know how you get on. And remember I am here to support your practice. Just message me at **ntathu@yogainspires.co.uk**.

Finally, remember to relax and spend at least 5 to 15 minutes every day practicing meditation. Choose one of the techniques outlined in this book, and try it out for the next five days. I guarantee you will notice a difference in how you feel and how you respond to situations.

Most important, be gentle, slow down, rest when you can, and enjoy each day of your life.

Namaste,

Ntathu Allen

BOOK DISCOUNTS AND SPECIAL DEALS

Sign up for free to get discounts and special deals on our bestselling books at

www.TCKPublishing.com/bookdeals

About the Author

Ntathu is a writer, yoga, and meditation teacher who inspires and supports busy women to experience more pleasure and delight in their lives. She offers simple, self-care yoga exercises and techniques you can do at home or at work to help you release worry, feel calmer, and be more creative and focused. Mother of three imaginative, young-adult daughters, Ntathu uses yoga to remain joyful, balanced, and healthy. She offers free blog articles with weekly subscriptions via her website.

Visit **www.yogainspires.co.uk** for your FREE guide download with video and audio: (**www.yogainspires.co.uk/subscribe**) "Get More Energy" 7 simple stretches to boost your energy.

YOU CAN ALSO CONNECT WITH NTATHU

Twitter:
twitter.com/yogainspiresyou

Blog:
yogainspires.co.uk

Facebook:
www.facebook.com/yogainspires
www.facebook.com/groups/breathecalm

LinkedIn:
www.linkedin.com/in/ntathuallen

Quora:
www.quora.com/profile/Ntathu-Allen

Instagram:
www.instagram.com/yogainspiresyou

Amazon Profile:
www.amazon.com/Ntathu-Allen/e/B0085F6XAI

OTHER BOOKS BY NTATHU

Yoga Basics For Beginners: A Simple Guide To Yoga For Beginners For Health, Fitness And Happiness
(Yoga For Beginners Guide Book 2)

Work Happy!: 26 Quick and Easy Relaxation Tips To Help You Breeze Through Your Day

Healing After Loss: 28 Devotional Poems for Healing and Peace
(Religion and Spirituality Books)

How to Love Yourself More: 365 Motivational Quotes & Affirmations to Kick—Start Your Day!

Back Care—Yoga Exercises for Lower Back Care at Work: Reduce Stress, Boost Energy and Improve Posture
(Stress Management Techniques)
(Back Pain Relief Treatment Book 1)

Mom and Me Have Fun Baking Thanksgiving Cupcakes
(Thanksgiving Book for Children)
(Children's Cookbooks for Holidays and Celebrations 1)

Do You Know If Kindle Unlimited Is for You?
The Ultimate Guide to The Benefits of Kindle Unlimited for Avid Readers

Mom and Me Have Fun Baking Thanksgiving Cupcakes

Love Your Life: 26 Inspirational Poems to Nurture Your Spirit Through Hard Times

Yoga for Beginners Your Complete Guide to Detox Your Body and Calm Your Mind

Visit Ntathu's Amazon Author Central Page to find out more…
www.amazon.com/Ntathu-Allen/e/B0085F6XAI

One Last Thing...

If you enjoyed this book or found it useful, I'd be very grateful if you'd post a short review on Amazon. Your support really does make a difference, and I read all the reviews personally so I can get your feedback and make this book even better.

Thanks again for your support!

www.ingramcontent.com/pod-product-compliance
Lightning Source LLC
Chambersburg PA
CBHW050044080526
44586CB00014B/1442